The Eightieth Year

The Eightieth Year

A Journal

Don Thompson

RESOURCE *Publications* · Eugene, Oregon

THE EIGHTIETH YEAR
A Journal

Resource Publications
An Imprint of Wipf and Stock Publishers
199 W. 8th Ave., Suite 3
Eugene, OR 97401

www.wipfandstock.com

PAPERBACK ISBN: 979-8-3852-1169-2
HARDCOVER ISBN: 979-8-3852-1170-8
EBOOK ISBN: 979-8-3852-1171-5

VERSION NUMBER 04/18/24

In Memoriam
Kay Marie Thompson
1943–1945

Artists are people driven by the tension
between the desire to communicate
and the desire to hide. . .
It is a joy to be hidden
and a disaster not to be found.

—D. W. WINNICOTT

Suzy Song: What do you want, the truth or do you want lies?
Thomas Builds-the-Fire: I want both.

—SMOKE SIGNALS

You wake up, some fine morning, old.
And old means changed; changed means you wake up new.

—RANDALL JARRELL

1

On the night train southbound to Hong Kong,
I heard the iron glossolalia
of the rails—
not Chinese or any human dialect
and not the tongues of angels.

It was black on black outside
as if that province were the low ground
darkness sinks to,
a thousand feet below light level.

The face no one wants to face
looked back at me from the window.

My wife slept uneasily,
upright on the hard wooden bench,
dreaming (as she still does)
of Xanadu or somewhere beyond.

I wanted her to wake up and tell me
what it's like in another world.

—

The old grove, dead and uprooted,
was chipped and hauled away
for fuel, for mulch—who knows?
Maybe for horse bedding instead of straw.

Now seedlings take root, or try to,
tentative in the cleared ground.
They seem withered already, dying,
and each clings to a white support
so that the new grove
would remind anyone of a cemetery.

But up close, tiny leaves shimmer
in the late afternoon
like fragments of lime sea glass,
jade pendants or neon green
uranium glass illuminated by UV light
that would make a Geiger counter chatter
with excitement.

—

Sparrows stick to business, diligent
among bread crumbs
the Lord provides for them from my hand.

No slackers in that crew
with its brown and tan uniforms,
struggling to meet
the exorbitant quota of calories
it takes to sustain such manic metabolisms. . .

I'm worn out just watching them,
sipping black coffee
to encourage sluggish blood
and get my mind back to work
pecking at its own crumbs.

2

Evening light only in the room,
no lamps lit. But enough
to illuminate
the fake gold leaf of a repro icon

that glitters on a shelf, leaning against
an inherited complete set
of the *Great Books of the Western World*
no one ever has or will read.

Whenever I open a volume, it creaks
like my joints, but audibly,
and the fine print of human wisdom blurs.

Also an off-brand encyclopedia
purchased decades ago with grocery coupons:
pristine obsolescence with a faint glue odor
that's outlasted everything we used to know—
that could be toxic.

My house is less library than book graveyard.
Paperbacks I've had since high school
that turn to dust if I touch them.
Titles I've always intended to read
and never will.
Others I want to reread once more—
once more, given time.

—

Here and there in the Mother Lode,
churches of all sorts, some unused—
painted and kept up,
but strip-mined of the Holy Spirit.

I parked on gravel and walked into a grove,
ragged light pinned together by pine needles.
And stillness—tangible.

The small church painted white on white
had a few windows I could peek through—
no stained glass on the budget,
unless flush, gold rush congregants
considered it popish.
And no pomp inside, only self-conscious
simplicity, determined not to put on airs.

No one ever wept in that church.
No one got the Holy Ghost and shook.
No widow ever looked up from her lap
into the eyes of a lonely shopkeeper
and no children squirmed.
Worship was a stiff backbone business.
No tambourines and no spurs
and no dust. . .

The pews had been waxed,
altar gleaming like a dining room table
in a Victorian domicile
with three Irish girls to keep it that way.

No doubt some old women from town
came monthly with rags and Pledge
and polished everything,

maybe without a word of local gossip,
then left, fastening a padlock
larger than a clenched fist.

Where I live, if I hold out my hand
dust settles on it. Time
sifts down onto the crepey wrinkles of my skin.

Must be synchronicity between them.

This place could be the bottom
of a vast hourglass
where time like dust and the dust of time
descend—a slow
but continual drift covering me.

—

Yes, but. . .
I'm here for now in my recliner, sipping
a few ounces of modest red,
content in dim light
to watch the icon glimmer—
gold leaf more and more authentic
the longer I look.

3

Dickinson must've been a bit—
witchy.

Not a vindictive hag
who threatens straw men
(like me) with fire,
who scares bats back to their cave
and makes an owl want to walk home.

Nor that crone
in every neighborhood in my time
whose grass is dead,
shrubbery withered to the bone,
whose curtains have been sewn shut
like the eyelids of a shrunken head.

No—but witchy nevertheless.

Imagine you live next door
with a path between her house and yours—
well worn, although
you never see Emily on it,
but find on your porch hothouse flowers
that burn your fingers
wrapped in notes so enigmatic
you'll never make sense of them
and never stop trying.

—

Where I grew up, outside town
among nut groves beginning to uproot
for tract hutches
in which to breed postwar babies,
I took ditch banks everywhere
instead of streets.

And once came face to face
with our designated neighborhood witch,
who never left her house
except to howl from the porch
when one of us had taken the dare
to cross her yard.

Flour sack dress, work boots I suppose,
hair like thick white smoke
too heavy to rise,
and over her shoulder—
a rifle. . .

Here memory's brittle 8mm film
disintegrates. Not to a black screen,
but white with the flash
of crackling synapses.

Maybe she just scowled
and went about her dark business.
Who knows?

But now I wonder if I frightened her,
if she'd armed herself
in defense against us, proto-men
who taunted her, who pelted
her roof at night with walnuts,

who couldn't leave her in peace,
needing, uncontrollably, mystery—
the frisson of witchiness.

—

Stairs steep and no wider than a ladder,
as I recall, entre to a hiding place—
Dickinson's room.

I could be looking into a dollhouse,
authentic floral wallpaper, tiny
furniture built to scale
by some mad craftsman who insisted
that details
keep the devil out.

The dress is repro, of course,
an unyellowed white with fussy pleats
and excessive buttons. Modest
doll clothes for Emily's "freckled bosom".
It stands upright on its backbone,
dignified and then some, appropriate
for a Victorian nurse, a nun, a ghost.

But I can think only of that headless mannequin's
fierce gaze that isn't there—
like Rilke's Apollo.

4

The half-dollar liver-colored birthmark
inside my right knee
has—almost—faded away.

Perhaps some sort of bio-chronometer,
factory installed.
A color chart came in the carton
to hold next to the birthmark
and estimate how much
time remains until it expires.

Lost long ago, of course.

Unless it's in that box of baby clothes
in my closet, relocated
from Mom's closet in her last house,
arriving there from earlier attics and garages—
a moveable time capsule,
never opened.

But that chart itself would be faded,
no more useful
than a wannabe gypsy's guess.
Something else outlived.

—

I knew an ancient woman once,
blind and not living
but barely existing with dementia.

Of the equine type,
never a beauty, but ravaged by then
like that abused cart horse
whose suffering drove Nietzsche mad.

She'd been a carny
or an original biker chick
with tattoos to prove it—
unthinkable otherwise in her time.

But that validation had all blurred,
leaving her arms
with crank case oil or blackberry juice
smears that made no more sense
than her mind. . .

—

Girls now will outlive their tattoos
and in old age, have to explain
to no one who cares
what those stains meant to them.

And remember looking over their shoulders
into a mirror to admire
above low-rise jeans,
that tramp stamp, freshly inked
on a tabula rasa.

5

Chestnut mare grazing in the morning sunlight,
Sunday morning, alone in the pasture,
her color precisely
that of my sister's bronzed baby shoes.

Memory more that fact, no doubt,
but why remember at all?
And why now?

Those shoes stood on a walnut platform
among the bric-a-brac of our house
for years, always dusted. . .

So when did Mom finally
put them away?

They must've been laced,
but I recall laces dangling
and the shoes agape—
tiny, hobo boots, broken down
by all the years of wandering,
homeless,
but always at my side.

—

In a blurred Kodak I cherish,
Kay's laughing

11

as she toddles, off balance
on one foot like Chaplin's tramp
skidding around a corner
and gone.

Other snapshots survive
and one studio portrait: head-tilted
pose they put little girls in,
mustard-colored jumper and blonde hair—
probably too blond, tinted
in this print by a hobbyist aunt
when coloring photos was a fad.
Like bronzed baby shoes.

I suppose another print sailed
on a slow boat to China
to the Kunming APO
commanded by tech sergeant Dad,
who'd never seen her and never would.

—

Grisaille memory, so old
it has to be in black and white,
flickering on a Cartesian theater screen.

Alone in the back seat, I look out
through the windshield at dark windows,
impenetrable, in a wall
of fog-colored stone.

Mom returns, without
a word to me or even a glance,
pounds her head on the steering wheel
and sobs, sobs
until the memory fades.

6

Dad indulged me, snapped
his son at fourteen
on a North Beach street corner
outside the Co-Existence Bagel Shop.

No need for self-mockery.

My canary yellow gypsy cart
'48 Chevy coupe
burned more recycled oil than gas.
I'd park near the edge of town
and hitchhike to the City—
trusting loose change and illusions
to get me there and back
before school on Monday morning.

No need. None.

Dad exiled me
to the house behind ours,
sacrificing rental income
to be unburdened of my attitude.
Black walls and fish nets,
candles melting in wine bottles
salvaged from a nearby tavern's trash bin—
and jazz vinyls.

Miles Davis *Round Midnight*
going round and round
in my head—
Coltrane's solos more vivid now
than first love.

—

Windows fogged for privacy
at the drive-in theater,
tinny speaker mumbling inaudible
dialog like rain. . .

No chance of that for six months.
And by then,
she would've moved on twice.

L.'s intense need had turned to alcohol
years before I saw her again—
a leathery husk,
aching for her confiscated children.

Refused the drink I would've plied her with
and looked at me like an ellipsis
she had no reason to fill in.

—

Sunday afternoon jam at the Bamboo Room,
empty, except for us
pet white boys,
refugees from the sock hop.

No need for self-mockery.

We huddled in a corner
and sipped Cokes from the bottle,
listening to locals blow old bop tunes
with a break now and then
while the trumpet man
slipped into the rest room
to shoot up.

And now I listen sometimes
to late Miles—the pimp get-up,
anodized trumpet,
that hair-plugged and gnarled mahogany skull.

Miles with more than enough said,
content to noodle in the groove.

7

Mom and Dad were in the wind
for two weeks every summer,
stashing me
at YMCA camp on the coast.

Fog sifting through pine needles overhead
and warm dust on the ground
to kick up shuffling to the mess hall.

Neither craft-handy
nor called to the playing field,
an only child loner,
I wandered
through the camp's tamed woods
(poison oak eradicated),
ending up on a sea cliff.
Out of bounds.

And hunkered down there in a concrete bunker,
an observation post
manned only ten years earlier
to scan for Japanese periscopes
across an empty and still empty
180° view of dazzling Pacific.

If it hasn't been jack-hammered years ago
as an attractive nuisance,
I wouldn't go near that bunker now:

Beer cans and condoms, graffiti
on the walls and in the air,
a fecal subtext.

—

Camp legend of a ghost
haunting a rundown, abandoned cabin;
rumors of a mountain lion
among us.
I could hear the deep huff
of her picking up our scent
outside the windows,
scritching on the bolted door.
And in the morning,
find footprints behind the mess hall
among tipped over trash cans. . .
Maybe.

In Edward Hicks' Peaceable Kingdoms
(pick one) the big cats
are just about to snap—
rigid, jaws clamped on rage,
eyes exophthalmic.

The children, mere dolls anyhow,
are in no danger,
though the trusting ox with halo horns
may not live to swallow that fodder.

But, in fact, the lion's staring out
at us,
an unmistakably hateful look
seen sometimes in a mirror. . .

Still so far from peace
with myself.

The camp packing list called for a Bible
and Mom retrieved one from a bottom drawer
among household dross.
Unopened until Sunday chapel,
at random,
while I fidgeted on a split log
in fog and dust, ignoring
an unhelpful homily.

And found in it a brief, fill-in-the-blanks
newspaper obit
along with a lock of wheat-colored hair
tied with a ribbon—
a sheaf harvested much too soon.

—

An impulse. Who knows why?
After stuffing my old suitcase
with dirty laundry
and buckling recalcitrant straps,
I gouged it
with my pocket knife cum lion claw.

And back home, breathlessly
told all about the night prowler,
the door barricaded with luggage,
and how the beast almost got through.

Mom and Dad went along with it—
acknowledging my close call
with a wink and nudge
that now seems so much like love.

8

That summer I worked graveyard
at a truck stop on 99,
mostly out in the scale house
reading Whitman under a bare bulb
so dusty and moth-encrusted
it cast only a dim light.

Things happened, I think.

Bought a suit from a drifter
for gas, no doubt stolen—
a heartbroken green and shiny thing
I wore once or twice
or less.

The Lovin' Spoonful in a Ford Falcon filled up,
silent, staring straight ahead;
and a French girl in a yellow Mustang convertible,
whose mini-skirt flustered me.

National Guard tanks on lowboys
among deuce-and-a-halfs loaded with troops
rolled slowly toward Watts—
just in case.

Things like that.

—

A kid from somewhere shot himself
parked along the roadside,
and our sling truck towed in the car,
blood-splattered interior already attracting
clouds of flies by sunrise.

Next night, the father showed up,
disgusted by one more mess
made by a son who'd messed up everything.

Hired two girls who hung around,
snubbed by truckers,
to do the cleaning for twenty each,
which they did—
easiest money in a long time.

Then something else happened. . .

—

Now and then the hippocampus
clams up, its gristly hinge
making sure the black half shells
fit together too tightly
to pry apart.

Outside, rough surfaces—
impenetrable.
Inside, for its own pleasure,
that nacreous glow
of the past.

No light seeps through.

9

Cool air makes promises it won't keep
in the thin dark, pre-dawn,
but still dark enough not to see the snail
and crunch it underfoot.

Autumn leaf sound in mid-summer.

Some regret—but not much,
considering that snails aren't innocuous
with their almost motionless
passive aggression, their soft animus.

Shredding the leaves of our ornamentals
like vandals keying a new car.

Swallows glittering with contempt
for us
slice the air, showing off
their knife fighting technique.

Nothing benign about them.

Their nests under the eaves
bulge like goiters—
the deck below plastered
with an impasto of dung.

—

After we poked their nest, hornets
swarmed from an abandoned chicken coop
and came at us hard and straight—
unwavering kamikazes.

Each one pure rage
contained in a drop of amber acid,
hatred that presupposes consciousness,
and focused
on task unlike my wandering mind.

R. and I stood back to back,
swatting them down with ping pong paddles
and never flinched, never got stung. . .

Hornets have nailed me twice this summer,
making me do a panic dance
I hope no one saw.

—

Skipping stones select themselves.
It's not your eye
falling by chance on one
the size and heft of a twenty dollar
gold piece gleaming in the mud.

No—that stone
attracts you somehow.

Gone mad from eons of sitting still,
it craves the lithic adrenalin
of flight—breathless skittering

across a lake only to sink
deep into deeper mud. . .

And in zen gardens of raked gravel,
it's obvious
that the stones decided for themselves
where to be placed.

The priests waited patiently,
as long as it took,
while the *ishi* made up their minds.

10

"Well," Mom said, "it's over."
And then the flat recital—
drone of grief that feels nothing
yet, synapses shutting down
to make pain less than unbearable
when it does come.

No wonder some of us never answer the phone.

Dad lay deflated on his back,
a tube still in his nose
that had let most of the air out of him.

Plastic pearl buttons on his western shirt
glittering in bluish fluorescent light,
toes up and one sole worn through
like that famous campaign photo
of Adlai Stevenson.

Dad voted for Ike
and died with his boots on.

—

Mom made oyster stew
to please him, though not often,
and served it in fluted cobalt blue glass,
two bowls never used otherwise.

I'd have Raisin Bran for dinner,
finicky at best, refusing
those nasal gobs in white paste.

And once on Vancouver Island,
the time a bald eagle
bent the tip of a pine like a fishing pole,
Dad prowled among tide pools,
prying oysters loose with his jackknife.

His awkward-looking rough hands
that took so easily to any manual skill
opened the shells, doused
each oyster with Tobasco sauce,
and tipped it down his throat,
one after another,
while the eagle and I admired his panache.

—

Dad's hands tossed into his lap
turned surly—rare zoo animals,
dangerously bored,
that had to have something to do.

In retirement, he puttered around
(as we used to say),
adjusting the drip line on his rock garden,
installing unnecessary gadgets.
Built redwood picnic tables to sell
on consignment at the hardware store.

And sculpted (I'd say now)
Adirondack chairs for the family,
all weathered away years ago—
except mine.

Parted out two others to refurbish it
like the ship of Theseus.
And whether or not it's the same chair,
it is—
if you ask me.

11

This cottonwood must have *Todestrieb*
(if you believe in that)—slowly
committing suicide by self-neglect.

The tree's retracted its roots,
giving up on possible deep water
below the slough
that's been dry for years.

Insects drill into its bark,
hundreds of test holes—
wildcatting for soft rot.
One limb withers
and one swollen limb will swell
until it splits.

And it's the same tree I saw a gray egret
lift off from a decade ago,
working hard to get airborne,
but graceful. . .

Others of its kind, leaves sparse
but supple and undeniably
some sort of green,
have felt their way down to the aquifer.
They get by.

—

Post-war, Dad healed himself
with his own hands—
became his own priest in a pith helmet
serving at the altar
of the house he was building.

Weekends and after work
as long as the light lasted on summer evenings,
mostly by himself,
with only a few sacramental tools:

hammer and hand saw's chant,
working through stacks of black market lumber,
green and prone to warp,
with only a mail order blueprint
for liturgy.

I remember a level at least three feet long
with chartreuse bubbles,
its brass and mahogany steampunk elegance
splattered with paint.

And a huge plumb bob in sync with all things.

—

Lines outward from our house
plotted on a mind map would've connected us
to five walnut trees
with roots deeper into earth and time
than anything I know of.

And those massive, overhanging gray trees
acted as *eminences grises*
of my childhood.

I'd lounge in the easy chairs of their limbs
for comfort
or to smoke a Lucky Strike
among the confidential leaves
and absorb their stoicism
from thick bark to thin skin.

12

Mom redecorated in her mid eighties,
took down those awful De Grazia
blobs of Navajo urchins
and put away anything turquoise.
So much for Southwest.

But cobalt blue Depression glass
made the cut, I think,
surviving on its own shelf,
backlit and glittering
bijoux in a mélange of styles—

though all the same exquisite shade,
so calm, so reassuring.
No wonder the Virgin Mary chose it
for her robe.

Fifties maple at first,
a bland neither-nor color, beveled
with outsized pseudo-medieval feet
that clashed with the chintz upholstery,
flounced along the edges.

And much later, matching leather recliners. . .
Dad died in his, laughing
at a bad comedy on VHS tape.

—

Post-beat teen newlyweds,
C. and I went with the original
Cost Plus look,
making a pilgrimage
to the Fisherman's Wharf store.

Closeted the plastic Venetian blinds
that came with our duplex
and hung bamboo roll-ups instead.
Grass mats on the floor.

I still have one of our plates—
bright yellow enamelware
on which we ate guacamole for dinner
with Fritos and Dr. Pepper.

—

At eighty, I'd rather not refurnish
my mind—
less bold than Mom,
who committed to late life change,
emigrating indoors from Southwest
to Provence.

Better to stay put and reread books
on the brick and board shelves
of the past,
at least those not literally
crumbling to the touch. . .

13

In Leibniz's era, the mind
compared itself to a mill—
cogs and wheels and pulley belts,
levers to do the heavy lifting.
But no evidence
of perception in all that machinery.

Now it's an au courant computer
that sorts and stores
yottabytes—memories
easily recovered, in theory,
if you know the keystrokes.

I go with the old house analogy,
rundown and occupied
by a half-mad recluse who hoards everything
and forgets it's there.

Bedrooms of grown up and gone children
neck deep in yellow newspapers,
eighty years of crisis
rather than cherished reminiscence.

Kitchen cabinets filled with stale cereal,
Kraft mac-n-cheese like boxes of rocks;
hall closets nailed shut
on the past, debris

of time's tsunami washed up in the living room.
Idols in the attic.

Also a broken down pickup truck
on blocks out in the yard. . .

God help the garage.

—

Even this early in autumn,
The walnut grove has turned the color
of junkyard rust—
Some green persisting here and there
like shredded vinyl seat covers.

Everything's metallic—
post-industrial and desolate rubbish.

Scrub brush like bales of oxidized wire.
Cottonwoods like twisted girders.
Plain dirt foothills in the distance,
drilled for oil but not mined,
make convincing slag heaps,
rubble that absorbs afternoon light.

A dangerous-looking landscape
with risk of tetanus worse than snake venom.

—

Stone and wood sculpture
come naturally from the earth at least,
if not as-is. Bronze
statues begin as controlled lava flow.

Trash art could be litter redeemed,
transfigured, I suppose,
or not—
just pretentious like pre-torn jeans.

Garbage in garbage out.

14

That old feed store south of town
could've been a tomb
if Pharaoh were a dirt farmer
who succeeded, whose son
shrugged off the city and came home,
an ag biz grad from Cal Poly,
and took over—

doing it all with computer models
and printouts analyzing soil
that dad ran through his fingers,
tasted, and tossed in the air
to catch its drift. . .

Tomb quiet in that store
and tomb dark,
most of the bulbs in the rafters burned out.

Fragrant hay bales, chicken mash
and feed for illicit fighting cocks
sold, but not much else—
less stock than artifacts on the shelves
that someone might've needed
but never did.

Imagine an archeologist in situ
with a brush she could've used for make-up,
delicately dusting

hundreds of mysterious oddments
good for nothing now
but a doctoral dissertation.

—

Lady intended to do me in—
without malice, though,
but simply to remove an irritation
from her back:
a six-year-old with a tin sheriff's badge.

Tried to scrape me off against the barn door,
hustling to her stall and her mouthfuls of hay—
no one to bother her
there in the dusty, vague light.

Grandpa's old pinto mare, lordotic,
overweight and world-weary,
with whom I empathize now,
always wanting only to get back
ASAP to my recliner.

—

Augustine walking on the beach
tripped over a tooth—a human tooth
that would've fit in a skull
large as the house I grew up in.

No archeologist to sign off on it,
of course. But why not believe?

Down the road from that feed store,
half of a gargantuan beer can

sliced lengthwise
flashed neon that said DANCE.

Tinny acoustics. Guitar licks bounced
and collided coming and going—
a Charles Ives effect.
Boot heels like hooves on the concrete,
women slip-sliding in stockings.

Mom and Dad would put me in a corner
among the shoes
while they drank and danced
to country legend would-bes. . .

Took Buck home once, six
drunks and me in the back seat.
Cats in a sack. Dad
ended up in a roadside rose bush,
but made it to work, hung-over,
and raw with scratches no one mentioned.

15

Fallen pistachio leaves—a dull,
almost khaki,
certainly not a color autumn advertises.
Soon they'll be silver-gray
like coins frozen in a heap,
so old they'd been rubbed smooth
before I was born.

Walking a dirt road beside the grove
every morning, I glean—
clumps too snug for harvesters to shake loose.
And I have a so-so eye for ripe nuts,
those gone beyond
green and subsequent carmine
to a color matching the leaves.

Peeled and their clamshells pried open,
always flavorful and sometimes,
if not often, slightly sweet.

—

The sun filtered by haze
in late October
is no harsher than the bulb
hanging above my recliner.

Not to be looked up at, of course
(150 watts of actual incandescence),
but reflected early this morning
in the gold leaf edged pages
of my Prayer Book. . .

A good light to be born in.

—

Found the family Bible last night,
overlooked on a high shelf,
brooding and reclusive,
less scripture than incarnation
of a black mood.

Holy Spirit lifted from it long ago
and now just dead weight, disintegrating
pages the color of those pistachio leaves,
cover board detached like a lid.
It's all come unglued.

Birth, marriage and death entries
mostly updated later, obviously
in Dad's handwriting less than fifty years ago.
That Bible just for recordkeeping,
heritage surviving
his temporary foxhole faith.

And no name blacked out.
So I was wrong. . .
Paramnesia?

But It's my past, after all—remembered,
misremembered and made up.

October 24, 2022

16

The great aunt who collected glass elephants
had watched rogue lightning strike
her best friend.

How the look in her eyes got haunted,
I guess, despite makeup—
mascara and Kansas City Red lipstick
that offended
small town community standards.

Smoked cigarettes and drank beer too,
sitting at the kitchen table with Mom and Dad
(taking a break from the abstinent farm)
while I contemplated the elephants
that emitted a poignant
light that never hurt anyone.

Shameless contrast with Nana
who wore homemade flour sack dresses
and blocky, square-heeled lace up shoes.
Doilies like confetti in the parlor
no one ever used,
living in the kitchen like Aunt M. . .
Something in common.

Dad broke his nose twice
playing football for the Yellow Jackets

back when rural high school games
were riots obedient to a whistle.

A release for farm boys feeling trapped
as unpaid labor in thrall to fathers
who worked both themselves and their sons
from dark to dark. . .

Dad escaped to California.

—

Visiting peanut farmers in Arkansas once,
relatives of some sort,
trying to fall asleep on the couch—
Calvinist furniture, scratchy and unyielding.

Sultry night, darkness that sticks to skin,
both dust and rain in the air, fifty-fifty,
and thunder coming closer.

Then from the wooden crank telephone on the wall,
lightning cackled
across the room and out the open window.

—

In the dark root cellar, refuge
from bipolar weather,
lightning and manic twisters
that missed the farm but hit town once,
and those glooms of summer heat
with humidity that closed in
like self-loathing.

Down there, Nana's garden crop—
string beans, corn and okra
put up for the winter
in Kerr jars that crowded the shelves.
Each gave off its own faint
and reassuring light—
just like those glass elephants.

17

Grandpa got up at four to milk cows,
the barn lit dangerously
by a kerosene lantern, hissing.
I went with him—once,
too used to keeping California hours.

He shot milk from an udder
into the mouths
of mouse-or-go-hungry cats
that tumbled over each other,
frantic to get at it.
I tried, but had no grip—
never did
and have less now than then.

Also sat in his lap on the tractor,
a no-nonsense John Deere—
guttural diesel chug, smokestack puffing black.
Its huge steering wheel's diameter
equaled my arm span.
Not a chance I could turn it. . .

Fabricated from leather and baling wire,
lean and fierce, Grandpa
lived in bib overalls and a straw hat
and died hard.
Men like that always do.

Too much will for their own good
like wild animals that kill themselves
chewing off a leg
to escape from a trap.

—

Old tractors so often die alone,
pushed off the field
after their last sputter, their agonal gasps,
and left to the bindweed.

Time turns even John Deere green to rust
and yet those massive, gnarled tires
never go entirely flat—
at least not in your long life
or mine.

—

Dad came up from the root cellar
with an heirloom, neglected
enough decades for that shotgun
to rust solid:
an 1890s Winchester lever-action 10 gauge,
which he brought home to restore.

He'd slip the noose of his necktie
and work on it evenings,
a civil servant's diversion from red tape.
Hundreds of hours until it was immaculate—
polished walnut, bluish silver-gray barrel
and action smooth as butter.

Never risked firing it though.

Less gunsmith than sculptor,
Dad wanted to put hands on his past
in order to recover from it
something tangible.

18

In old age, just to put socks on
exasperates—
inflexible body, intractable mind.

Heels dry up and crack in cold weather.
That hurts. Nails thicken,
rough as fresh water mollusk shells.

Morning limps are hints of mortality,
even if you loosen up later
under the sun. . .

And sometimes, I suspect that death
comes in through weary feet
like those nematodes
that worm their way to the heart—
horrid little angels of doom.

—

In the Dead Sea Scrolls of insomnia,
a few footnotes
confirm my own experience.
Galen had physics for sleeplessness.
And some scorched fragments of parchment
that survived at Alexandria
offer sensible cures that still don't work.

Nothing has changed. . .

Last night my night train pulled off onto a siding
and sat there.
I'd hoped it would rock me to sleep,
listening to the rails murmur
their simple, repetitive prayers—
glossolalia without an interpretation,
but soothing.

Meanwhile an endless slow freight crawled by,
boxcar after empty boxcar
with now and then some sleepless drifter
staring out at me
with a takes-one-to-know-one look.

—

And if you fall asleep at last,
an inept sleep though,
as if you had no skill and not much practice,
then dream and believe
the dream in which you're lying awake—
such sleep will never refresh you.
You'll stumble through the next day
aphasic with gritty eyes
and flesh like mud.

19

The moon's drifting off west by northwest
this morning, white
as a burned out incandescent bulb
still screwed into its socket
behind cobweb thin clouds—
heaven's porch light
some shiftless angel forgot to change. . .

You can see why people think the place
has been abandoned.

Walls originally an intense blue
like the Virgin's robe
have faded to gray.
A mistake to paint them that color,
knowing it would never hold up
in harsh light.
In the long dry seasons of the heart.

No windows in heaven,
of course. No one's allowed
to look in or look out.
Only a door—one door
almost no one bothers to knock on.

—

The creeks Dad used to fish for trout
and bring back a few to skillet fry
on the campfire, rainbow
skin crackling and still iridescent—
those creeks look like cattle trails now.

The Kern River's a rock garden—
Zen in its randomness,
every stone precisely where it belongs.
Only a trickle remains of the rapids
that rampaged down the canyon,
too loud to talk over.

Remember that?

Mississippi down to a few sips
of its old self. Colorado
dribbling through a canyon on Mars.

The rain dancers are faking it,
naphthalene aroma on their feathers
and brittle leathers
last unwrapped before they were born.

And somewhere in the back of the Prayer Book,
a request for moderate rain,
irenic showers.
But that's not enough. . .

We need twenty feet of snow
in Donner Pass,
still melting in mid-summer.
Pray for ski bums on the slopes in July.

—

Maybe that Heraclitean river
we're so obsessed with
really is beginning to run dry.

Slow trickles slip under rocks and stay there
or disappear into sand.
Or find somewhere hard and hollow
to form little pools,
corresponding to memories, I suppose,
already layered with green scum.

Some places you can step into twice.

2 O

Leaves in a dry autumn turn brittle,
crumble to the touch. And yet,
seventy five years later
that sycamore leaf I took to kindergarten
show and tell
remains intact in memory.

Huge with a petiole thick as my fingers.
I held it up to my face
and vanished
behind its mask—translucent
in unsentimental classroom light,
amber fading into grenadine.

Magnificent,
if you're not embarrassed to say so.

Who knows what I said then.
Kids now would call it awesome
like Starbucks baristas approving
your choice of latte.

—

"I skipped church to water the corn,"
Dad wrote, 19
and living with in-laws in California,
who cultivated a de rigueur Depression garden.

Dug ditches for the water company all week
and dreamed of Mom,
finishing high school down in SoCal.

Just a chit-chat letter,
somehow preserved in its envelope—
nothing special
other than mention of a ring
and a five dollar bill slipped in
for a round trip bus ticket.

It fell out of the family Bible
along with assorted funeral brochures
and clipped obituaries. . .

Time's detritus.

Written in faded pencil
on both sides of unruled paper,
yellowing into its own late autumn.
Dad's nondescript script
concludes with a row of I-love-yous
followed by a footer of solid Xs.

—

Mom and Dad went to church
only on biannual visits to Kansas—
going along to get along.
The bland Methodist-Episcopal pastor
made no threats from the pulpit, reaffirming
the town folks' sensible midwesternism.

Nevertheless, they snuck off afterwards
for a beer

from their stash of Pabst Blue Ribbon,
Kansas being dry on Sunday. . .

A beer to rinse away the stringent taste
of Charles Wesley's hymns.

21

This memory's as old as I am—
almost, anyhow: postwar
when we lived in a shackish little house
among walnut trees, patriarchs
standing around us in a circle.

And it's not on film, but slides
kerplunkinng one by one through the viewer.
And those not in Kodak color,
but shades of brown—
sepia come by honestly,
not a fake antiquated look.

I was sick—undiagnosed,
feverish with paralysis creeping up my legs.
Mom and Dad stood by, helpless,
with a lost daughter in their eyes.
The house-calling doc had nothing in his black bag
but stethoscope and mercury thermometer.
And penicillin.

Shot me up every day
until I began to get better, finally
wobbling out of the brown shadows
one morning, bright and clear after rain,
sunlight glittering in puddles. . .

Looks like I'll make old bones after all.

—

Keeping an eye on the Elk Hills—
not to watch for peace
which comes down from high mountains,
according to a psalm,
but for righteousness that's within reach,
that descends from the hills.

Not so far. . .

Today the chariots of the Lord
could clatter down those slopes
and no one would notice anything,
the haze so dense—
a gray curtain with hills showing through
like mauve shadows.

Last night I saw scattered oilfield lights
that always remind me
of the cook fires of an invading army.
And above them in a starless sky,
a slice of lunar rind
tossed aside by a homesick angel.

—

Six years old with a bone
to pick with Dad,
I threatened to run away and did.

Apple, socks and agate shooter
wrapped in a bandana on a broomstick,
I walked off in the dark—

twenty minutes into eternity
and once around the block,
the entire world as I knew it.

22

We're well into decrepitude,
the year falling apart.

Too late to glean pistachios,
shriveled and hard now—
handfuls of gravel
behind leaves beginning to let go.

Their pale green's reminiscent
of insane asylums
abandoned before I was born
and no doubt haunted,
their walls faded to that color.

Anyone would want to throw rocks
at the windows of a place
of so much suffering.

But all the glass is long since broken.

—

Gloom like pig iron weighs us down.
Cheerfulness has no more heft
than feathers.

Nevertheless a pound's a pound,
so it's possible for the scales to balance. . .
If not now,
maybe in the long run.

—

Check the gas and fill it with recycled oil—
that '48 Chevy coupe Dad bought me
for fifty dollars.
Painted it canary yellow
in honor of Toad's gypsy wagon.

Dad's new '59 Biscayne
that I left unbraked in neutral
rolled downhill for a block or two
and into a net of shrubbery.
No harm, no foul.

Volvo fastback that threw a rod
near mispronounced Cholame,
going half the speed
of James Dean's Porsche Spyder.

'53 Cadillac Coupe deVille, aging
but indomitable and still stylish
that I drove to group therapy sessions
at Sonoma County's mental health clinic.

'65 El Camino that no one else loved
and the '55 Chevy two-door post,
powder blue like the boudoir
of a mistress—
also too expensive to keep up. . .

A junk yard Cerberus watch dogs
every ossuary of dead cars
and the wrecked dreams that died with them.

Chained all day, he's let loose
to roam at closing time—
silent and much too mean to bark
before he bites.

23

Two or three mourning doves
breathe softly into pitch pipes
to make sure they're in tune
before sounding their one note.

Sparrows somewhere out of sight,
but nearby, chatter at random—
an a cappella choir gossiping
until the conductor taps her baton
and they shut up.

A crow clears his throat
as if he could actually sing
if he wanted to,
but decides to listen instead.
Even crows can be humble.

—

Although without levers, the wind
knows all the tricks of heavy lifting.
It can take off a roof all at once
or shingle by shingle.

Wind can snap an oak in half
and bring it down.
Lightning can only crack it.

This afternoon clouds run from the wind
as if chased, dumping
their load of rain to pick up speed.

No birds in sight—
not so much as an old raven
with his curmudgeon attitude
that usually refuses to seek shelter.

I take that back. . .

Under the panicky, shredding clouds,
a hawk hovers, face to the wind,
holding its own like a kite
on unbreakable string.

—

On the radio—seventy years ago?
Canaries carried on for an hour
every Sunday, I think, their warbles
accompanied by saccharine violins—
each obsessed with its own song,
ignoring all others and the music.

I've been told those birds were faked,
just people whistling. . .

But I don't believe it.

24

Rembrandt's cow, ruminating,
ignores the coming of the Lord
in that quick-sketch brown ink Annunciation.
And the torturer's horse,
scratching his itch in Auden's museum,
has no concern for human suffering.
Our ecstasies and pains bore them
winter and summer, autumn and spring.

And yet horses bear us as their burden,
more or less willingly,
until they drop.
Cows provide milk every day
until they go dry
with only an occasional complaint,
lifting their heads to bellow. . .

Nothing's easy for any of us.

A trustworthy old plug limps to the glue factory;
a cow, harmless as anything in this world,
bows her head to the bolt gun.
And we sometimes end up toe-tagged
on the coroner's slab.

—

Nevertheless—Good News!

Those shepherds out in the hills looked up,
gob smacked by myriad angels
singing praises to the Lord
in a key unknown on earth—
x sharp or y or z flat.

And here's a plastic crèche to remind us
of the actual manger—surrounded
by hard scrabble sheep herders
and random lice-pickers off the streets,
merely curious;
by a lame horse, a withered cow,
a couple of sheep in a dither,
and an off ox.

And here's my ceramic Tannenbaum,
one of Mom's gewgaws.
Lord, may I live to plug it in
a few more years, at least—
faint light in primary colors
pushing back against darkness.

—

During a break between sets
at a local hotel's lounge, access allowed
to underage jazz fans
who sat on exhibit in a corner
behind velvet ropes,

I went in search of Sonny Rollins
and found him, brooding
alone in an empty banquet room.

Post Ryker's Island and Lexington,
just prior to the Bridge,
who knows how touring out West
brought him to our town.

I asked him to autograph a cocktail napkin.
He did, without comment,
and I withdrew. . .

Not yet thirty, almost Aztec features
carved in lignum vitae.
Skull cap hair precisely the opposite
of his cotton ball Afro at eighty.

Even jazzmen wore dinner jackets
with black bow ties back then,
and his was a fierce white—
illuminating that dark room
like the bare bulb you see
on an empty stage.

25

Coyote's scat in the dirt road
indicates hard times—
that he's eaten something indigestible
and been caught short.

But this mess with blood in it,
a bit like stewed plums,
represents only a temporary setback.
Coyote will be fed.

The hound that usually barks
when I walk by
gave me a pass this morning,
no doubt in his doghouse
curled tighter than a sow bug.
His kibble will keep.

Tentative ice on the horse's water.
But he's got his woolly mammoth coat on,
snorting for alfalfa cubes
and a carrot.

I feed him and then crumble dry bread
for the sparrows
you can count on to show up,
noticing that the dead mouse
I tossed from the porch yesterday

vanished overnight—
fed on.

—

Although dry, the field's black
and already pre-furrowed
for next spring.

If you think about it,
even the soil will be fed,
slowly masticating decomp—
leaves and grass,
branches the wind snaps off,
any dead creatures scavengers miss.

Us too, you could say—
sooner or later, no matter how well
our leftovers are packaged.

—

Lord, receive this, my aubade—
my lauds
offered not with incense smoke
but with breath clouding.

Let me continue to be blessed
with the cold
that burns my double-gloved fingers
and humbles me;
blessed with breath
that I can see so clearly as it vanishes.

26

Nothing repairs the cracks
in your heart
when love parches to hardpan.
Lips too dry to kiss dry lips. . .

Think of those ephemeral lakes,
less than ankle deep like our affections
and quickly evaporated.

The curse of self-salted earth.

Sun glare on the lakebed,
miles and miles of shimmering white
worse than snow blindness.
And fissures every which way—
chaos, crazed filigree
without intuitive spider web design.

Alkali might conceal,
a wind temporarily fill,
but nothing ever closes them—

except another wet season
of shallow flooding,
caliche turning to mud
and all the fractures collapsing
in on themselves.

—

Auden had to recant, of course,
since so many of us live well
without loving each other
and reach narcissistic decrepitude.

He himself aged badly, dying
younger than average at 66
with a centennial face:

classic hound dog eyes, tight-lipped
and cross-hatched with wrinkles,
his skin once so pale
in the end like white mud
dried, weathered and liverish.

—

Insane or foolish? You decide.
Or is it audacity
to go on into old age
dissembling with capped teeth,
living in hair plug denial,
holding on to love's empty bucket
by its handles?

It takes good DNA to grow old gracefully,
accepting the descent
with no more than a cautious grip
on the stair rail
and allowing your limp to set the pace—
a largo tempo with accents
on the upbeat.

Remove the cheese cloth filter from the mirror
and own your wrinkles.
Let your yes be yes, your no be no,
and your gray be gray.

27

Even before the knees' cheap hinges rust,
before muscles relent
and that famous grip on jar lids slips;
before testosterone dehydrates
and long before yesterday, today and tomorrow
end up in the same junk drawer,
indistinguishable,
before all of that, the will goes lax.

Nietzsche's boxed out in the garage
along with avant garde French novels,
surrealist dream slag and Maslow.
Next step the thrift store
and unwanted there, on to the landfill.

Paperbacks crumble, dust to dust.
Those seedy offices of noir gumshoes
are for rent. No takers. . .

Things just don't get done anymore.
Cobwebs in the corners,
surfaces out of sight never dusted.

Under the unpruned snarl of the elm
in the backyard, leaves
molder that I must confess
will never be raked.

—

Someone else I never could've been
wins the door prizes
I never won
after sitting through a lifetime
of vindictive banquets,
listening less to speeches
than to the tin click of fake silverware
and ambient Spanish chatter
from the kitchen.

That man does well, even does good—
an upgraded Doppelganger
who holds the patent on a quiet mind
and cornered the market on balm
from Gilead.

When he dies easily in his sleep,
his tally will earn him
a virtuous unbeliever's ticket to Limbo.
And ferried across the Styx,
he'll offer Charon a tip,
laying his solid gold cufflinks
on that calloused palm.

—

A stiff northwest wind
caroms off the back of our house
and shifts due east,
leaving the oak out front
in the lee—for once.

Huge and old, it's been battered
from every direction.

But calm now, holds out bare branches
and shows them to me—
both of us
bemused by how still they are.

28

Laudate Dominum—always the best option,
choosing to praise
rather than grumble in my tent
and sip tepid coffee,
rancid with cream of chagrin
or laced with bitterness,
if not Irish whiskey anymore.

Even if euphoria keeps eluding me
like an angel
who cringes at the sight of such gloom
without cause—my face
with its default frown
that's merely a bad habit after all.

Did Mom warn me to cheer up
or I'd get stuck like that?

Or did I assume her expression?

The inward turn of mind,
the clamp-down and noncommittal eyes,
the sealed lockbox of how she really felt—
so much trapped behind clenched teeth
and then swallowed.

"When Dad growled," she said once,
"I tossed him a bone."

—

The raven's baritone klaxon
conveys no emotion, not really—
neither all-purpose complaint nor boast,
neither Sartre's nausea
nor the mock gag of schoolboys
confronted with dance class.
Close to that, though.

But it does get my attention
and makes me look up:
a huge bird with pry-bar beak
and raucous rather than arrogant
like a hawk,
but equally imposing.

He's the single, polished totem
of the carpe diem clan,
with no other carvings below him,
perched on a power pole
that has no patibulum—
only the cable that brings overpriced
light into our house.

—

Nut trees stand in the wreckage
of last year's illusions,
strictly pruned
as Scripture says we all must be—
though we'd rather grow unhindered
in wild directions.

A crew's been in this grove for weeks,
going home at night with sore arms
from lifting long trim poles,
those little guillotines;
necks crimped from looking up.

And they earn such meager wages,
doing the Lord's work.

29

Might as well be nuclear winter
for the ants, gone underground
into silences deeper than their own silence.

Their empire has fallen, anthills leveled
and not one grain of sand left on another.

Waiting it out in their simple refuge,
they sleep until radioactive frost melts,
antennas waving slowly
with an inner awareness that never shuts down.

Meanwhile the bunkers of the elites
remain empty, but ready—always ready.
LED glow, lullaby hum of air-conditioning
and every surface surgically clean,
linen crisp, larders full
of survival food with an infinite shelf life.

Ready and waiting.

—

My shell's hard but thin
and brittle.
With a carapace of glass,
I need to hide—vulnerable,

so easily shattered by circumstance
no matter how long I buff it
to get that unconvincing sheen.

A gimcrack effect, after all, typical
of shoddy goods.
Authenticity has patina—
mottled and streaked, a bit greasy,
its finish worn down over the years
by a worried thumb.

Bric-a-brac me.

Consider the vintage Hummel figurines
behind glass in our dining room
that we should've unloaded
back when they were overpriced.

Compare those with an old man's talisman
I saw on TV, a genuine silver dollar
carried in his pocket since boyhood—
rubbed blank as a planchet.

How many times lost and found?
And yet he takes it with him everywhere he goes,
everywhere his heart goes.

—

Shadows like mold spread across the ceiling
of the shopping mall,
half the lights turned off now.
Empty shop windows covered with butcher paper
keep making their false promise:
OPEN SOON.

Potholes in the road no longer annoy us,
nor dead grass in the meridians.
Parks could be old battlefields
littered with needles instead of shell casings.

And in the overgrown rose garden,
a plaster saint, paint chipped,
raises a hand hand less in blessing
than to warn us away.

30

Last of the late January persimmon sunrises.
A clear morning, although without clarity,
clouds in a holding pattern
off to the northwest,
waiting for stragglers to drift in
before making their move.

Showers predicted later, but rain
if it does fall,
will be only a footnote
referring to an earlier deluge
already half-forgotten—
by us
and by the soil
that's begun to crack again
into familiar jigsaw pieces—
a closely fit picture of plain dirt. . .

Winter grass—yes, and succulent.
But in a landscape that's comprised of
six or eight shades of gray and brown,
it's hard to believe in.

And yet, in this windlessness,
bare trees seem to shudder
as if feeling a green itch.

—

Scripture alludes to God's warehouse
in which storms are held for distribution,
angels with clipboards
keeping tabs on the inventory.

Not high-tech, but efficient,
and He's had no labor unrest
since Lucifer. . .

Metaphor rather than meteorology,
but it makes more sense
—to me—
than a young woman in front of a blue screen,
who's not quite chic, chattering
about isobars and inversion layers.

Our TV weather lady back when,
less scientist than skeptic,
obviously doubted her own predictions.
Dowdy and schoolmarmish,
she stood behind Plexiglas and wrote
backwards on it with a grease pencil.

—

This finch would be a nonentity,
as drab as I am,
if not for his vermillion cap.

He's fluttered from frosty branches
to perch on the sill
and peck at his own image in glass,
making a racket.

Always an undeniable early sign
of spring, of spring foolishness—
wasted on me, of course.

And irritating—like some Romeo
tossing pebbles at my window
by mistake:
Juliet lives next door.

31

Somehow reprehensible to turn the world
into words, as if
you could come up with a rhyme for napalm
and not hate yourself.

Body bags should zip up less flesh
than silence. . .

Even Sassoon, scribbling in the trenches
a hundred plus years ago,
licked his pencil stub and knew better.

Knew that actual gas
would be reduced to a leitmotif;
that in the end, everything he lived through
would lie dead in anthologies—
no more than irony eliciting a nod.

—

Down in the hippocampus
or wherever records are stored,
electric impulses
could be written out in longhand
and fill thousands of volumes—
octopus ink on parchment between vellum boards,
each titled in gold leaf.

For just one unremarkable life like mine.

Not to mention all the historical addenda
to memory, perused
by the file clerk who works nights in that library
under a bare bulb
with his old school, green plastic eyeshade.

Just names. Some exotic,
some euphonious and some absurd—
Tenochtitlan, Antietam, Tarawa, Ypres
that only survivors were allowed
to call Wipers.

Places never meant to be
depositories of anonymous bones
with no Ezekiel to reassemble them,
but all synonyms for slaughter.

—

A mountain lion asleep in lavender
will let you pass.

Rattlesnakes resent snake grass,
so beware. They'll be moody.

Never look twice at a vulture
or make eye contact even once.

Anyone who dreams of barracudas
needs our prayers.

No moon rising over a battlefield
is bad news. Always.

But never resist feeling encouraged
by moonlight on frost.

Your inner sumo wrestler is a friend;
your inner ninja—not so much.

Blessings and warnings are one,
so take both to heart—and live.

32

A thousand years may be less than a day
for God, but for these gaunt hills,
eons take eons to pass.

Most of their soil's been eroded, leaving
a thin skin over bedrock.
But I notice
new grass evangelizing the slopes,
greener as it goes higher. . .

Eightieth spring for me,
an incalculable number for the hills—
lush again,
except for gullies and gravel patches
that remain barren like scars.

—

I know a place that specializes in light.
Nothing's quite like it anywhere else
so that I wonder if it's our sun
or imported from another
more distant and more scintillant star.

It's unique light, a new genus
with salt in it—a sequin sparkle
spilled across the dry lakebed.

Anything that grows nearby,
in those years with rain,
withers quickly
after blossoming with weak colors—
chartreuse grass, lemon-yellow poppies
and lupines no bluer than faded denim.

And yet, it's effect on us is counter-intuitive,
enhancing our urban moods.

I'm content there
and always leave with a residue
of salty light on my hands
that I don't want to wipe off.

—

Somehow the old oak's caught wind
of spring—
bare limbs alert, poised for
renascence not yet perceptible.

I'm unconvinced, though,
still thinking in terms of mud
tracked into the house,
of wicked low temps every morning
and numb fingers so hard to warm.

My blood's sluggish like winter sap.

Nevertheless, I suspect I should yield
to the oak's experience,
although it's only a decade older than I am,
planted in the early 30s,
a few twigs swaddled in burlap.

And besides, year after year,
when spring finally does come,
I'm slow to believe it.

33

Cold morning. Retro weather
with frost in the fields
and unexpected ice
to bust through on the horse trough.

A few miles south, mist
follows the course of the Aqueduct.

An indeterminate white smudge on the hills
that should be wildflowers,
something common
with a ten syllable scientific name,
is actually thin fog—a desperate
effort to revive winter.

Too late.

The hills are committed to green
although higher up
the I5 is iced-over and closed
until the sun can get to it.

And no one will pick up the bee boxes
already stacked next to the orchards,
even if the bees refuse to come out.

—

Early in spring, ghosts
send their vestments out to the cleaners—
some threadbare, some recently unwrapped
with Indonesian sweatshop tags,
some with original French designer labels
and a few of the side hustle brands
of Hollywood stars.

So many—so many dead
of all classes, of all tribes and tongues,
that it takes until autumn
to get it all back.
Just in time for haunting season.

—

Between here and sunrise, night
falls like black curtains, hundreds of them—
some plush velvet, some gauze
or seamless linen;
maybe even biker jacket leather
lined with satin
or 18mil, heavy duty body bag vinyl.

But all black.
And cold to the touch.

They muffle sound so much that a dog
barking nonstop on the next farm
is barely audible,
as if infinitely distant—
life signaling from another galaxy,
even lonelier than this one.

34

On an unpaved, dead-end road
beneath massive walnut trees,
remnants of an orchard,
we sat tight in a house without bedrooms.
Mom and Dad unfolded a Murphy at night,
and I slept on the couch.

The pre-war washing machine
on a screened porch
had a ringer that could crush an arm—
a beast Mom warned me to watch out for.

Laundry fastened with clothespins,
heavy and functional
rather than chichi paperclips,
dried on taut lines
between oilfield pipes welded
to form a Greek *tau*.

That makeshift home was dark inside,
a Rembrandt interior, shadows
offset by shades of ochre, umber and sienna.
The old linoleum had assumed the color of dirt,
and the only, almost-bright surface,
the kitchen counter, remained
a lead-tin yellow long since outlawed.

Grim. . .

But Dad had a plan—blueprints
ordered by mail
and breathing space among the trees
he could build on.
And did.

—

Some still wear their heart on their sleeve
or at least tattooed on a bicep.
Others have their heart up on blocks
out in the yard, weeds
sprouting around it like loose sutures.

They'll sit on porch steps that sag
until the sun goes down
and the beer gets warm, listening
to an old radio
with vacuum tubes that glow in the dark.

That high-lonesome Appalachian tenor
would break their heart
if it weren't already broken beyond repair.

—

I've always been autumnal,
my moods making the most of earth tones.
October born.

Some years unripe, acidic green
sets my teeth on edge
or pollen debilitates me.
And yet I'm not opposed to spring.

Late February now. Almond trees
have started to blossom,
beginning with lower branches
like can-can dancers flashing their lace.

Kind of exciting.

35

Love ought to be pinned down
on black velvet—
an iridescent cobalt butterfly
with a label leaving no doubt
about taxonomy.

Even so, we'd insist on common names:
Vagabond, Gaslight, Nemesis,
and so on. . .

And if you look up love
in the heart's thin dictionary, half-blank
with coffee stains on the unused pages
and so few definitions you can commit to,
you'd find only double-talk
and sophistry.

Nevertheless, something irresistible in us
blushes and stammers
when we try to speak its name—
familiar as a moth,
more exotic than a blue morpho.

—

My tent predates nylon
in those manic shades of blue and orange,

hi-tech designs
that set up by themselves.

Suitable for climbing Everest
or a homeless camp.

And my tent's canvas, war surplus
khaki, stiffened with water proofing
that by such close association
has made me inflexible.

Worn to cheesecloth in some places,
ripped and stitched,
guy lines frayed and pegs loosening,
it won't last much longer. . .

But I recall its dusty aroma
on warm afternoons, and how sunlight
softened inside without casting shadows,
and lying there beside another
in such a cherished illusion
of intimacy.

—

Every bird's somewhere out of the rain,
except a raven near my upstairs window
swaying on a power line.

His croak has suffering in it—
two or three more turns
of a wooden screw.

Looks like he's been stood up.

But she's just late, finally
fluttering down beside him
with all the time in the world.

Now the raven begins his courtship,
an awkward bird, too eager
and without savoir faire—
wings half-flapping like the elbows
of a vaudeville comic
doing his impression of a chicken. . .

Desire's so absurd, nonsense.
Who needs it?

And yet we all pirouette, soft shoe and two-step,
caught up helplessly
in our own mating dances.

36

This zoo should be and soon will be
shut down. Its keepers
no longer care
and rare visitors sneak in
without paying the fee.

Grizzled specimens with milky eyes,
a limp and two or three teeth—
Avarice, Wrath, Envy
languish in unlocked cages.

A silver back alone in the gorilla compound
has that dirty-old-man look in his eyes.

A widowed polar bear ambles back and forth
beside a pool of toxic water.

No birds sing in the aviary
where everyone admired their dazzling colors,
delighted by their happy clamor.

And the snake house is knee-deep in sloughed skin
with a few boas in the shadows
that never show themselves.

—

Some words have been dead for so long,
unburied and picked over
by scavengers,
that they've become anonymous bones
and mean nothing to us.

Other words like Victorian
ball gowns, all crinoline and tulle
and frustrated lace,
adorn manikins in the museum
of silence.

Emily Dickinson's little white dress
still speaks to us,
but in words too enigmatic to make sense.

And that homeless guy I talked with last week
spoke brain-fried gibberish,
a dead language,
trying so hard to tell me something.

—

Thunderbird, that sour lemon cologne
blended with hair oil
gleaned from half-empty bottles on skid row;

and Red Mountain in a glass jug
with a handle you could hook a finger in
and drink from it over your shoulder;
we all slummed with those brands.

Mom and Dad's bourbon
you could safely sip two ounces from
and replace with tap water
without diluting its shade

of wild honey amber with sunlight undertones;
we all did that.

Our bottle of Id so hard to keep the lid on
with that girl who never drank;
and her mother,
always with gin and tonic at hand—
a slice of lime, precisely
the color of lust;
no one I know drank with her.

Single malt Scotch with impossible names
that twisted your tongue
unless you drank enough to loosen it;
moonshine in a Mason jar with no label
and all the brands, so familiar,
everyone's born knowing who's born a manchild
in this thirsty, inebriate land.

37

Light makes a painstaking exegesis
of the grass, the new grass,
comparing it with ancient manuscripts—
papyri that survive every winter
down in the monasteries of the roots.

And there's no doubt now
that this green is authentic,
that this is, at last—
spring.

Even the blackbirds sing hallelujah,
sort of, their yellow eyes
somewhat less malevolent than usual.

Not a hint of leaf buds on the trees,
not yet. But soon.

And then, descending,
instead of a genteel dove with an olive twig,
swallows that get right to work,
building their mud hovels,
excreting concrete.

—

Regret never lets up, does it?
Not so much the drunk at a party
you can't shake,
violating your personal space
with his beer breath, his bad puns
and stories you've heard hundreds of times.

But more like that excruciating prof
who lectured from the text
and never looked up. . .

I know that if I returned to school
after decades of hard knocks,
he'd still be there with his head down,
reciting the *Book of Things Gone Wrong.*

—

The old bull stands firm in the past,
archetypal, although I moved on—
back across wet pasture grass,
through barbed wire, and drove away. . .

Almost sixty years down the road now.

That afternoon the bull looked up
from his salt lick
and made eye contact with me,
a stray trespassing hiker.

Skin shivering with disgust, he snorted,
considered attack,
but laziness outweighed rage
in that thick skull, for once,
so he let me go.

And here I am.

38

I claim Celtic monks in my DNA,
scribes and translators,
along with vicious little maniacs
who painted their faces blue,
on back to hordes from the steppes
who fought on ponies
so short their feet dragged.

I've got genes from Visigoths
who sacked Rome
and even from land-grabbing Normans
mentioned in the *Domesday Book*.

Mongrel me. . .

The pie chart assesses 2% Jewish,
less than a dollop
to offset one quarter German.
Those immigrants hunkered down in sod houses
on the prairies and survived,
speaking less English than the wind.

Otherwise, nothing of much interest,
no off-the-grid ancestors,
African, Asian or indigenous—
just a bucket of Scots-Irish blood
spilled across Appalachia.

—

That sound inside your head when you eat ice,
loud enough to suppress thought,
or rifle shots
of ice breaking up on a distant river
far north of any emotion
I'm willing to feel.

And once on a hotel balcony in China,
the city obliterated by acrid smoke,
I heard fireworks crackling nonstop
like synapses overwhelmed
by one thing after another.

But most of all, in a complicated summer,
clouds of dust-colored
grasshoppers settled on our town,
crunching under tires until the streets
were smeared with yellow paste. . .

You could look into your empty coffee cup
and those black eyes would look back,
lifeless but alive,
famished jaws grinding.

—

Rags flutter on the thin branches
of my family tree—
only remnants of tattered generations
and not easy to identify.

Gray cloth with bone buttons
and blue with brass.
More shreds of denim than any other fabric.

A straw hat with no crown,
leaving a halo for an angel fallen
into hard times.

A scalp.
A moonshine jug on a string.
Something that could've been a lacy black bra
might be withered, parasitic vine.

And for leaves, imitations
snipped from copper,
every bit as green as actual foliage
after all these years.

39

The doc's thermometer beeps and reads me
at room temperature.
Post mortem.
He frowns, resets, tries again,
and brings me back to life. . .

Nevertheless, I distrust digital,
remembering mercury
on those cold, inhospitable mornings
when I claimed fever.

Mom's no-nonsense snap of the wrist
warned me not to be faking
before she slipped the thermometer
under my tongue:

metallic taste and the risk
of glass between my teeth
that might shatter;

then a solemn minute's wait
for the result, knowing
that unlike anything now,
it would be final.

—

Three coins: 1942 Mercury dimes
with the image of that winged,
busybody god,
still not rare in the sixties.

I shook them like dice in cupped hands
and tossed them to calculate
a hexagram.

We all had copies of the *I Ching*,
interpreting in our California manner
all that ancient mumbo-jumbo
that meant—whatever.

One girl wore peasant skirts
and carried a tarot deck in her purse.
Another drank Southern Comfort
straight from the bottle.
Both soon moved to San Francisco.

My hexagram said stay put.

—

Now and then in the quicksilver past,
some kid would crack open a thermometer
and bring mercury to school—

for the real show-and-tell at recess.

You'd coat a dime with it, bare-handed,
and delight in that brief,
insane shining
that faded eventually to dull pewter.

But for days, I suppose,
that coin would be chrome—
refulgent, catching light
like a pampered '32 Deuce coupe's bumpers.

Who could live long enough to forget that?

As a codicil, I ask
that one of my bones, a femur,
be dipped in mercury
and displayed among hubcaps
on a junk yard wall—
too high for the dog to reach.

40

Is Yeti actually out there, a vague
entity lumbering back and forth
across the interface
between *is* and *could be*?

A shadow on ice, a snowdrift
with fierce black eyes
focused on the empty landscape
of nonbeing—

a footnote in some editions of reality,
but left out of others.

Clumps of fur snagged in brambles
come back from the lab
with a shrug—DNA unknown.
And indistinct footprints
comprise the only facts on the ground. . .

Who knows?

And yet Yeti's no more mysterious
than diminutive Emily in a white dress
brooding among the Himalayas
of her own solitude.

—

Sometimes I sit here glum
in tattered safari khaki and a stained hat,
thirsty and discontent, scorched
by the sand of my personal Sahara.

Sometimes I refuse to move. . .

But just over the dunes
in any direction,
the ashy gray sand, redeemed,
sparkles like benign ice.

Palm trees as far as anyone can see,
their fronds touching,
swayed by winds that arise
somewhere eternal
and maintain an ambient 70°F
throughout that infinite oasis.

—

They stuffed Ruth in a discount coffin,
the most lifeless shade of gray
with a rip in it
like a booth in an all-night, skidrow diner,
and buried her without ceremony.

So long, friend I never knew. . .

But once I snuck into the off-the-grid
rest home after hours
with cartons of fudge ripple she craved.

Rolled her wheelchair along indifferent hallways
to the empty dining room.
No security back then.

Toothless and obese, snarls
of thin, demented hair—
a mess, but giddy as an ingénue
on her first date,
she gobbled all the ice cream
with her pinkie finger extended.

41

The heart's plumb bob never hangs straight down,
but contra naturam, swayed
toward love's magnetic pull
or repelled by it,
yields to its own inclination.

Mine's been replaced by a wooden weight,
nonresponsive one way or the other—
true to gravity at last. . .

But I remember car windows fogged
in August, end of summer
desperate in the back seat
at a five-dollar-a-car drive-in theater.
Wanting to know that I knew.

And then, decades later, holed up
in a spidery room
with cash skimmed from a failed business
and excellent whiskey, listening
to my post-divorce share of the vinyl.

Contented with solitude, somehow—
heartbreak's unexpected spin off.

—

A dog's barking tonight
at least two farmhouses from here—
so far and so faint
that I have to hold my breath to hear it.

This must be how the past sounds
down in the limbic system, howling.

Listening I think of that Baskerville hound,
bloodhounds on the scent of an absconding felon,
a gangbanger's pit bull
with his studded collar and bad attitude,
mascot of some Gestapo squad
or the archetypal junkyard dog. . .

And I know, even at this distance,
the past bites.

—

Grandfather oak's in full leaf now,
except for the dead limbs.
Another broke off in the wind last week.

The elm we ought to have pruned
has lost its balance—
an insane snarl of wandlike branches
almost touching ground,
overloaded with panicked greenery.

Mid April now
and the dwarf orange tree's wearing pearls.
That wicked little pomegranate will bear thorns
but no fruit again this year.

And the faithful mission fig hides
behind modest leaves,
already lifting its unripened prayers.
These will be answered.

42

After a downpour, sitting here
in soggy introspection,
the field outside the window reminds me
of elementary school finger painting.

A rainy day activity—as reminiscence is now.

All my primary colors smeared to mud
gray, thick paper dissolving
on my desk
while I hesitated between crude images—
some sort of quadruped, a tree
or a stick figure boy sinking into that bog.

A mess for the custodian
to scrape off with a putty knife. . .

Gao Qipei limned his Eagle and Pine
with long fingernails.
I'd approximate a turkey with my handprint,
then wipe it away,
aware that it was infantile.

Why that compulsory self-expression,
that crazy-making therapy?
I wanted only to be left in peace
to doodle fighter planes
gunning each other down with dotted lines.

—

The wind's one of those impressionists
who can do any celebrity voice
the audience calls for:
Sirocco, Chinook, Mistral, Santa Ana,
haboob hurling sand out of the desert.

But they all sound the same in the end.

The wind this afternoon's no fake, though,
whistling through clenched teeth—
thin and hostile invective that stings.

It's been blowing for hours, bothering the trees
and bothering me—an unwelcome drifter
you'd willingly buy a Greyhound ticket
if he'd just move on.

—

Somewhere a wannabe saint
looks into his closet, deciding
which hair shirt to wear—
passes on camel and old goat
with a porcupine quill collar,
settling on a loose weave burlap.

We're all getting soft.

An off-the-grid eco hermit
low on propane
has had it up-to-here with asceticism.
The desert's too dark and the stars too far,
but Las Vegas glowing on the horizon

lures him—an easy
two hours in his camper van.

We're all getting soft.

Me too. . . And what a relief
to see that taskmaster in the mirror
give up with a shrug,
turn his back and let me be.

43

In the obsolete liturgy of a loose tooth,
the celebrant in his pajamas
ties a string around his incisor
and the other end to the knob
of an open door,
which he must slam himself.

Deus vult.

The ritual's invalid
if he stands there with eyes clenched like fists
and his little fists trembling,
mouth agape
while someone else does it. . .

I never had the nerve, but worked
a stubborn tooth back and forth until it let go—
a bloodied chip of faux ivory
that under my pillow overnight
would be transfigured into a shiny dime.

—

Neural network or not, something's
pre-transistor about me—
as if my wiring
actually consisted of copper wires

soldered together with the smoke and sizzle
of retro thoughts.

A late Marconi baby, the last
vacuum tube generation. . .

Reluctant to sleep, I listened
to my warm brown radio whisper
in the dark, comforted
by its tubes glowing
with unique light that no longer exists.

—

"No one knows how long a pistachio
can live," A. told me just before he died—
too young.
A male tree in Turkmenistan has roots
more than a millennium deep.

Early this morning, I walked
beside his—his widow's grove
and considered the April leaves,
a splash of sunlight on each one

like visual cologne
that comes in an infinite variety
of shimmer, glistening, dazzle,
each leaf with its own illumination
like every one of us—
like everything in the world
when sunlight anoints it.

44

Neon—neon everywhere back then
on every sort of business,
in colors the old masters never heard of,
making a terrifying, reptilian hiss.

And those overwrought marquees
with incandescent bulbs chasing each other
around and around.

World War II surplus Klieg lights
recycled for advertising,
wobbled back and forth in the night sky
whenever the new cars came out
or some tatterdemalion circus passed through town.

You can imagine how offended
the moon would've been
by those crass, crisscrossing beams
so unlike the glow poets used to get off on.

Not the moon as it is now, downgraded
to unnoticed ambient status,
but a deep sea bioluminescence
or a flashlight with weak batteries
held by someone lost in the woods
who's come across a trail
and has just enough light left
to get home.

—

Legends of an only child,
fitted together from bits and pieces
of uneventful solitude.

A quiet home with curtains closed
and emotions curtailed.

No squabbles over toys,
no elbows outside the bathroom,
no blood on the Monopoly board.

I've heard of such things. . .

In our neighborhood on the edge of town,
one actor grew up—almost B list
with a jaw line that could've cut paper.

A Korean War vet blew himself up
in his garage when gasoline fumes
reached a water heater pilot light.

Two brothers languished in their yard,
held prisoner behind chain link.
We talked through the fence,
living plain lives—
ordinary lives, in fact, all absorbed now
in the mythical gray flannel
haze of the fifties.

—

Morning light stuns whatever it touches.
Even a wren, unsteady on a low branch,

takes a standing eight count,
recovers, then flits away.

I'm sitting on the porch, lethargic
in Dad's Adirondack chair
with eighty years of gravity
in my lap
and enough hard knocks to cauliflower my brain.

Not so easy to get up.

The oak overhead has a decade on me
with plenty of dead branches—some attached
and some set aside in a stack for firewood.
But it boasts impervious bark
and leaves so green they'd shame a sapling.

OK. I'm up—
not as quick as the wren,
maybe, but on my feet.

45

The hills have shrugged off spring
and returned to their depressing
default monochrome—color
without a name.

Maybe a shade of dirty sienna
like the pelt of a lioness,
sick and out of her mind, caged
in a rundown roadside zoo
somewhere on Rte. 66 seventy years ago. . .

In our time, they'd close the place down,
lock up the keeper,
and euthanize the suffering beast.
Then try to forget the look in her eyes.

No wonder nobody likes it around here.

—

In my dream, my dreams ended—
ended, but not with the gut punch
of consciousness
that brings you back to this world gasping.

Nor with blindness when the screen goes white
in that inner Cartesian theater,

the dream obliterated in a moment
with nothing left
but the slapping of broken film
as the reel spins out of control.
Not that either.

Not like a shallow grave night prowlers dig up
and empty, scattering remains
across half an acre;
and not like a bottomless pit that finally fills,
silted over a lifetime
with detritus of countless dreams.

More like a recall—
my dreams all stripped from the shelves,
as if contaminated
with potentially fatal bitterness.

—

No one can escape
the mind's intricate hall of mirrors,
not even if you try to shoot your way out,
shattering all the illusions.

Rita Hayworth tried that and failed,
alluring but all wrong
as a tightly permed blond not really
from Shanghai.

And Rita failed off-screen too, love
always splintering like glass. . .

You have to find the exit
the hard way,
in and out of dead ends, confronted

by your own panicked image,
or coming up behind yourself
over and over again until something clicks
and a mirror becomes an open door.

46

In some medieval Ascensions,
the outsized bare feet of Jesus
poke from a cloud,
surreal and a bit goofy.

Down below, witnesses look up
in awe, their knees buckling.
But none of them giggle
as we tend to.

More serious about clouds that might
hide the Mother Ship,
we imagine it not sleek but steampunk,
crisscrossed with pipes and valves
and emitting an intimate glow
like blue love lights.

Up there, extraterrestrial gynecologists
examine abductees
and collect reluctant sperm samples. . .

Clouds are still clouds,
but the *Weltanschauung* has shifted.

—

This afternoon, the wind blowing
one way and then the other
irritates the trees that have to flutter
according to its whims.

Clouds that were here earlier
shuffled back and forth, knocking heads
until they finally dissolved.

Doves have gone to ground somewhere,
but one obstinate crow,
balancing on a power line,
keeps getting ruffled and then smoothed
and then ruffled again.

Me too.

This could be eschatological,
a prelude to irrational weather.
You have to wonder about a world
where the wind no longer knows
which way to blow.

—

You can look up into the sky
but not through it—
haze like murky water nowhere near
limpid. Dust
on the surface of deep space.

In this model, humanity
must be the bottom feeders—
predators skulking under rocks
that strike in a millisecond,
cephalopods uttering ink,

schools of tiny fish with wicked teeth
devouring each other. . .

But here and there, someone bioluminescent
drifts among us, untouched
by the madness.

47

This ditch has been empty for years,
drought years, all the water weeds
dead, brittle and assorted earth colors
as if some weekend Rembrandt
had been cleaning his brushes down there.

Now it's inches from overflowing—
high sierra evergreen green verging on black
and still cold enough to know
it's not local water.

Silver ripples filigree the surface
like a memory
of snow banks and pine-scented air
none of us have breathed for a long time.

—

Venusian glow penetrates the dust and haze,
but not much else. No stars to speak of.
The crescent moon's belly up and blurred
as if worried by a dirty thumb,
so dim it won't last until midnight.

No one falls in love under a moon like that
in air so toxic,
in a time so dissolute. . .

Maybe love's like one of those businesses
Closed For Remodeling
with windows black as this sky
and a few chips in the paint
where light shows through.

Somebody's in there working late,
hauling away fixtures and the last shopworn junk.
Everyone knows it'll never reopen.

—

A good year: the trees loaded
with nuts the color that bears their name.
Some already have the eager blush
of ripening.

Unseasonably cool this morning, sunlight
blessing its chosen leaves.

No reason for gloom in the grove. . .

I try to console myself with thoughts
of insidious fungal rot,
mold that crumbles roots,
or a cloud of locusts
stripping the trees bare.

But it's no use. I'm happy—
and I'll just have to admit it.

48

Massive walnut tree remnants
of a primeval orchard
with slabs of chalk-colored bark
like shiftless tectonic plates.

We had three of them in our yard,
and I'd sit for hours in a crook of their arms,
elders who instructed me
in that only child's isolated self-comfort
no one with siblings understands,
not quite. A knack
for keeping the mind too crowded
for loneliness to slip in. . .

Paleolithics would've worshipped those trees—
and why not?
Plotted them as points of a scalene triangle
with our little house enclosed
in its sacred space.

—

My head keeps humming nonstop
with tinnitus
like the inside of a conch shell
down here on the floor
of a drained Miocene ocean.

Or maybe it's more like putting on earphones
to listen to my own thoughts,
Radio Free Me,
and hearing nothing but static.

But the wind's silent. So far.
I feel it and see
branches weighed down by summer leaves
still waving goodbye to someone
who's been gone a long time.

—

At fifteen I wore my hair short,
as I do now—but thin and white
rather than the color of dusty dead grass
on the unmarked grave
of the past.

In this snapshot, I notice
a slight resemblance to young Teddy Roosevelt,
but bookish and a bit wispy,
posing like Truman Capote but hetero—
half-crazy hetero.

I hold an unfiltered cigarette,
contemplating the smoke
a la New Wave French cinema,
and lean back against a wall,
tangled in the fishnet that hangs behind me
without knowing it.

49

Polygraph the amygdala, interrogate
neurons until they snap,
subject frontal lobes to the third degree,
flood all your electro-chemical circuits
with truth serum,

but you'll never get to the Truth—
never point to a blip on the screen
or a spike on the printout
and say: There it is!

Leibniz could've told you that in 1714—
and did, in fact.

Truth clings to the circumference, the fringe,
conceals itself just beyond the tree line
where it's only a shadow
in deep shade.
You think you see movement,
a flash of eyes.

Or Truth's like those flowers
that bloom and wither and bloom and wither
in the cracked walls surrounding
an abandoned mansion.

Something in us insists on
throwing rocks through the windows
of a place like that.

—

A hawk shoves through the air,
graceful and determined,
but slow—ignoring two wrens
that keep harassing him.

Notice how the birds like fighter planes
attacking a bomber
avoid his weapons, beak and talons,
and dive only from behind and above. . .

Contra naturam, though, that predators
should be pursued by prey.

And I identify with one or the other,
depending on where I happen to be
on that sliding scale between them—
chagrinned hawk today,
vindictive little wren tomorrow.

—

Up north in those long-drawn-out winter nights,
warmed by fire and nourished
by whale blubber, an excellent brain food,
mythogenesis comes easy.

Not down here.
Local legends don't add up to much.
It must be the climate,
where some minds survive

but none flourish,
that parches the imagination. . .

After perfunctory mischief, Coyote
lopes away with his head hanging.
Scrofulous and underfed,
he'd rather get his teeth into something
that still has blood in it
and then sleep without dreams—
at least none to remember.

Like me—except for the blood.

50

This afternoon, thin-skinned clouds
huff off toward the south
to loll above a beach somewhere—
Costa Rica for all I know.

The wind gets on their nerves too.

The elm outside my window
self-flagellates for no good reason.
But this wind, this fault-finding wind
makes us all feel guilty.

One recourse is to sit tight
and wait it out. Try not to think.

This evening just before the light fails,
the wind will quit rattling my windows
and trees will finally settle down,
beginning to heal.

—

One odd year I worked the graveyard shift
along with the moon,
with nocturnal predators and cops
who love the night for its dissimilitude
and adrenalin—CHP,

who'd pull into the truck stop to gas up,
so itchy in their unflappable khaki
and friendly but always alert,
those happy owls.

Lex noctis states:
Nothing good happens after midnight.

For a few dollars, I accepted
a cheap stolen suit from a drifter,
which almost fit—
a color you'd call hopeless olive
with a greasy sheen.

I'd climb up to wash windshields
on big rigs, which reminds me now
of the woman who stepped in front of a truck—
such self-loathing to choose that death,
splattered like an insect
on the chrome grill of a Peterbuilt.

—

Looks like I'll make old bones after all,
packed, as is our custom,
in a shipping crate without an address.

You could toss mine among Yokuts bones
still turned up by plows now and then,
or into one of those red barrels
loaded with Chinese ivory
back when their cemetery was subdivided.

It's all good,

although I'd prefer that rickety platform
common among tribes on the Great Plains,
easy pickings for birds of prey
too lazy to hunt.

Or even a grave with a short-term lease
from which my bones would soon be evicted
and added to an ossuary.

But I'll pass on scattered ashes.
The wind's so fickle
that flakes of me would settle somewhere
I never wanted to go.

51

Empty shelves now. That drug store
in downtown Gilead's run out of balm—
nothing to sooth remorse
or take the sting out of bitterness.
No aromatic tears from the mastic tree
to cancel our tears.

A hand-lettered sign in the window,
black marker on cardboard and all caps,
blames broken links in the supply chain
along with dwindling supplies post-Covid
and post-Nietzsche. . .

Some of us tough it out, suffering,
but others accept
substitutes offered by Big Pharma—
feel-goods from the lab
that use up surplus consonants
to create names no one can pronounce.

—

Anger's our inheritance—rage
older than we are
singing an ancient dissonance
with those rhythms our blood responds to.

I hear wooden drums, bronze drums,
Caribbean steel drums and tin drums,
drums made with human skin,
snare drums of the Third Reich
and hollow logs echoing in the rain forest.
I hear cartoon gorillas thumping their chest
and my own heart pound.

I hear tympani in the temple of the amygdala
calling us to worship—
to gather there alone
and howl.

—

Not much chance I'll die in Venice,
asphyxiated by toxic canal fumes
while the golden lion of St. Mark
looks the other way.

But if I do,
seal my ashes in an urn
with a Tintoretto blue glaze
and decorated with punch drunk angels
that want so much to get up
and go another round.

52

The heart's a homeless encampment,
isn't it? Bedraggled
affections and affectations everywhere,
cluttering sidewalks that used to be
swept clean in the morning.

I am my own detritus.

And yet, my friends, will you
or any of us ever get off the streets?
Sleep in a bed with fresh linen
or think clearly?
Sit down to a meal that's not for freeloaders?
Receive love that isn't panhandled?

Or will we go on drifting?
Like grocery carts that pass in the night,
loaded with flotsam
salvaged from a thousand sunken dreams.

—

Kyrie eleison.

Christe eleison.

Kyrie eleison.

—

Eco-activists despise cotton
for its shameless thirst.
I know. . .
But it comforts me, reassures me
with its patient acquiescence—
straight rows knee-high now
as they should be in mid-summer,
blessed by sunlight
and water.

When my birthday comes around again,
with me or without me,
the leaves will be coppery
in a star field of cotton balls
ready to pick.

Of course I think of slaves,
photographed with long white sacks
and desolate eyes.
But also of those elephantine harvesters,
each with its solitary mahout
listening on earpods as he works
to the norteño top forty.

And I think of that first Neolithic,
no doubt a woman,
who stuck her thumb in the dirt,
dropped a seed into the hole
and watched it grow and grow. . .
and grow.